LIKEABLE LEADERSHIP

Hello and welcome to the second reflection journal in the Likeable Leadership series. The elements presented here are found within the Likeable Leadership series. The first journal focused on elements of self in the leadership journey. This second journal focuses on how your actions set the tone for your interactions with your followers.

To be considered a leader, we must have followers. In friendliness, positivity, availability, and practicing good listening, we establish a psychologically safe space for our followers. A week of reflection is developed for each of these topics in Journal 2. Each day includes a spot for three priorities and three gratitude memories. This daily practice helps us de-clutter our mind from worry and anxiety while strengthening our propensity to live a joyful and grateful life. The last page of the journal offers a space to highlight your favorite activities to carry forward in your leadership journey.

I am grateful you have chosen to share your time and energy on these pages as you continue your leadership journey. This space is designed for your development. For more in-depth readings on these topics, please visit www.strengthinnature.com. If you have any questions, kindly contact me at Angela.Buckley@creativelyefficient.com.

Yours in nature,

Angela

If found, please return to:

Name: _____

Address: _____

Phone: _____

Email: _____

Month started_____

TABLE OF CONTENTS

*Friendliness creates a space of psychological safety with a sense
of warmth. Are you creating a safe space for your followers?*

*Positive in leads to positive out. Setting the tone for each day
with a sense of positivity infects your team positively.*

*Influence is greatest in change and leadership when you are
available and present for your team. Are you scheduling
availability each day for your team members?*

*Good listening includes actively asking questions, approaching
topics with an open mind, and curiosity. Are you listening to
understand your team members' needs and desires?*

*When you have completed this journal, use this page to highlight
what you have learned and what actions you will put into
practice in one concise location. This page is your reference.*

Likeable Leadership Elements

1. HUMILITY
Humility is the art of valuing other people and their opinions, thoughts, and needs without indulging in self-pride.

2. GENEROSITY
Generosity is the spirit and action of freely giving to others. It sometimes refers to the overall spirit of kindness.

3. INTEGRITY
Integrity refers to aligning your actions with your words. Many people consider integrity to be "what you do when no one is looking."

4. CONSISTENCY
Consistency refers to being reliable and repeatable. Actions that are consistent are seen as fair and accurate.

5. FRIENDLINESS
In leadership, "friendly" refers to being beneficial or to serving a helpful purpose. "Friendly" combines with an air of warmth and kindness.

6. POSITIVITY
Leaders create the environment around them. The daily approach brings energy and sees the positive outcome to each challenge and opportunity.

7. AVAILABILITY
Leaders are available and responsive to those around them. Time is an important element of leadership when referring to availability and responsiveness.

8. GOOD LISTENING
Listening is a skill that hears both spoken and unspoken words. A true leader hears the body language, understands context, and asks probing questions to seek understanding.

9. FOCUS
Focused leaders concentrate on a particular aim, not wasting time, effort, or energy on other things. Focused leaders are present and work in the moment.

10. CELEBRATION
Likeable leaders laugh and celebrate successes. They work hard to support the team and they play hard to celebrate the joy of life.

11. HONESTY
Likeable leaders are open and sincere. Their words and actions are free of deceit.

12. AUTHENTICITY
Authentic leaders are human and acknowledge their mistakes.

HOW TO USE THIS JOURNAL

WEEKLY THEME →

CIRCLE DAY OF THE WEEK ↘

ENTER DATE ↓

FRIENDLINESS

S M T W (T) F S [ ]

>> Friendliness is a hallmark of servant leadership. We demonstrate the people are important by a simple handshake.

↰ FOOD FOR THOUGHT

⌐ DAILY PROMPT
↓

How do you greet the room? How do greet each person in the room? Can you balance friendly and timeliness in the meeting?

DAILY THOUGHTS

SCRIBBLES

DOODLES

⌐ WHAT ARE TODAY'S...
TOP THREE TO-DO

⌐ I'M THANKFUL FOR...
DAILY GRATITUDE

☐ _____
☐ _____
☐ _____

☐ _____
☐ _____
☐ _____

FRIENDLINESS

S M T W T F S ☐

>> Friendliness is a hallmark of servant leadership. We demonstrate the people are important by a simple handshake.

How do you greet the room? How do greet each person in the room? Can you balance friendliness and timeliness in the meeting?

TOP THREE TO-DO

☐ _____

☐ _____

☐ _____

DAILY GRATITUDE

☐ _____

☐ _____

☐ _____

STRENGTH IN NATURE
Leadership Series

**FRIENDLINESS**   S M T W T F S ☐

>> There are so many facets to the word "positive": compassion, energy, reinforcement, or even a kind word.

People gravitate toward warmth. Today, learn one personal fact about the members on your team, such as their favorite vacation or the names of their children.

TOP THREE TO-DO

☐ _____
☐ _____
☐ _____

DAILY GRATITUDE

☐ _____
☐ _____
☐ _____

FRIENDLINESS

>> Close working relationships often result in friendships. These relationships need space to breathe, forgive, respect, and love.

Friendliness also requires forgiveness. Do you easily hold grudges? Do you remember, recall, or focus on past wrongs? These burdens cause negative energy. What one past event can forgive today?

TOP THREE TO-DO

☐ _____

☐ _____

☐ _____

DAILY GRATITUDE

☐ _____

☐ _____

☐ _____

FRIENDLINESS

S M T W T F S ☐

>> Strong leaders demonstrate friendliness by advocating for their employees and teams.

Research shows that bullies can be stopped simply by standing near their victim. Do you stand up for your employees? How can you be more friendly simply by sharing your presence?

TOP THREE TO-DO

☐ _____

☐ _____

☐ _____

DAILY GRATITUDE

☐ _____

☐ _____

☐ _____

FRIENDLINESS   S M T W T F S ☐

>> Curiosity is an element of friendship. What more do you want to know?

The art of small talk is challenging for some. What are three phrases you can use and put into practice to engage others in conversation?

TOP THREE TO-DO

☐ _____

☐ _____

☐ _____

DAILY GRATITUDE

☐ _____

☐ _____

☐ _____

 **FRIENDLINESS**

>> Friendship is based in respect. When conflict inevitably arises at work, maintain respect and friendship, and argue about facts – not people or emotions.

Conversation is deeper than small talk. When is the last time you had a deep conversation with a team member? Can you make it a point to engage at least once a week in conversation?

TOP THREE TO-DO

☐ _____

☐ _____

☐ _____

DAILY GRATITUDE

☐ _____

☐ _____

☐ _____

FRIENDLINESS

» We express openness to friendship through body language. Our smile is universally one of the most identifiable messages of friendship we can send.

Life is hectic. We concentrate on work. Sometimes our faces reflect the stress. When conducting a meeting, do you consciously smile? If you are nervous in front of a group, what trigger can you create for yourself to remember to smile?

TOP THREE TO-DO

☐ _____

☐ _____

☐ _____

DAILY GRATITUDE

☐ _____

☐ _____

☐ _____

>> You can do this. You can lead. You can create a vision. Are you dreaming big enough?

Our positive attitude begins with ourselves. You are worthy. You are where you are supposed to be. What is one lie that you tell yourself that you need to debunk today? Believe it. Create your personal mantra.

TOP THREE TO-DO

☐ _____

☐ _____

☐ _____

DAILY GRATITUDE

☐ _____

☐ _____

☐ _____

POSITIVITY

» Bring positive energy to your day and everyone around you will reflect it. There is no better mirror than your children or your followers.

Your vibe attracts your tribe. Practice your positive mantra for yourself today and every day this week. What other step can you take to be more positive?

TOP THREE TO-DO

- ☐ _____
- ☐ _____
- ☐ _____

DAILY GRATITUDE

- ☐ _____
- ☐ _____
- ☐ _____

>> Acknowledge the challenge. Name the hardship. Then, channel your positive energy toward the solution.

In difficult situations, you can circle your team and intentionally pump positive energy into them if you remain focused on the good. Identify the silver lining in one difficult situation from the last few weeks.

TOP THREE TO-DO

☐ _____

☐ _____

☐ _____

DAILY GRATITUDE

☐ _____

☐ _____

☐ _____

POSITIVITY

S M T W T F S

>> Mirror the actions that make you feel comfortable so that your followers also feel comfortable.

Positivity is a daily practice. If you are uncomfortable, start with something small. Practice greeting everyone with a smile. Look for ways that you are comfortable with to make another person feel welcomed in your presence. Write three points here.

TOP THREE TO-DO

☐ _____

☐ _____

☐ _____

DAILY GRATITUDE

☐ _____

☐ _____

☐ _____

STRENGTH IN NATURE
Leadership Series

POSITIVITY

>> Optimism creates an energy that feeds all around it. Strong leaders know how to create positive energy, even in the face of adversity.

Facing a challenge with positivity creates confidence in your team. Positive thinking and courage are contagious emotions.

TOP THREE TO-DO

- [ ] _____
- [ ] _____
- [ ] _____

DAILY GRATITUDE

- [ ] _____
- [ ] _____
- [ ] _____

S M T W T F S ☐

>> Generosity is one way to spread positivity. When we give, we offer comfort and show that we are confident in the ultimate outcome.

Remember generosity of spirit? What about positivity in your heart? How are these two concepts related?

TOP THREE TO-DO

☐ _____
☐ _____
☐ _____

DAILY GRATITUDE

☐ _____
☐ _____
☐ _____

>> The word "positive" includes a sense of confidence as well as kindness. Do your interactions with the team increase their self-confidence?

How does your positive attitude influence others? What positive action can you take today to impact those around you?

TOP THREE TO-DO

☐ _____

☐ _____

☐ _____

DAILY GRATITUDE

☐ _____

☐ _____

☐ _____

POSITIVITY

S M T W T F S

>> Generosity, confidence, and positivity are easy bedfellows.

Why do you want to be a leader? Do you accept the sacrifices and discipline that come with leadership?

TOP THREE TO-DO

☐ _____
☐ _____
☐ _____

DAILY GRATITUDE

☐ _____
☐ _____
☐ _____

STRENGTH IN NATURE
leadership series

>> Emotional availability and understanding are important characteristics of leadership.

A likeable leader is available to their teams. Are you available in body and in spirit for those around you? How can you balance personal boundaries and still be available?

TOP THREE TO-DO

☐ _____

☐ _____

☐ _____

DAILY GRATITUDE

☐ _____

☐ _____

☐ _____

AVAILABILITY

S M T W T F S ☐

>> Being accessible is more than an open door policy. It is taking the
time to hear what is and isn't being said.

What does the word "available" mean to you? Responsive? On-call
24/7? Followers will seek leadership in a leadership vacuum. How can
you provide that leadership?

TOP THREE TO-DO

☐ _____
☐ _____
☐ _____

DAILY GRATITUDE

☐ _____
☐ _____
☐ _____

AVAILABILITY

S M T W T F S

>> Availability is one part listening and one part guiding someone from venting to seeking resolution. It requires patience and tact.

When is the last time you simply sat with a friend or colleague who was struggling? Can you focus on being available and bringing the energy of caring without forcing words or conversation? Can we be available and silent at the same time?

TOP THREE TO-DO

☐ _____
☐ _____
☐ _____

DAILY GRATITUDE

☐ _____
☐ _____
☐ _____

AVAILABILITY

S M T W T F S ☐

>> Serving others requires our presence and availability.

Availability has two components: physical and emotional. Leadership requires us to delve deeply into ourselves. What about leadership attracts you to serve others?

TOP THREE TO-DO

☐ _____
☐ _____
☐ _____

DAILY GRATITUDE

☐ _____
☐ _____
☐ _____

STRENGTH IN NATURE
Leadership Series

>> Presence includes managing our personal energy when talking and listening to others. Are you aware of the energy you give when you listen?

As a leader, we must share our knowledge and our talent. What one time management technique that works for you can you share with one person this week?

TOP THREE TO-DO

☐ _____
☐ _____
☐ _____

DAILY GRATITUDE

☐ _____
☐ _____
☐ _____

 **AVAILABILITY**

>> Availability means we can bring our strengths to bear so others can benefit.

Leadership does not have a specific recipe for success. What is working for you right now? How can you capitalize on your strengths?

TOP THREE TO-DO

☐ _____

☐ _____

☐ _____

DAILY GRATITUDE

☐ _____

☐ _____

☐ _____

STRENGTH IN NATURE
Leadership Series

AVAILABILITY

» Beyond office hours, beyond open-door policies, be present in the moment; be available.

In our world of immediate access and constant interruptions, how can you be available and present in the moment? What is one specific action you can take to balance presence, private time, and availability?

TOP THREE TO-DO

☐ _____

☐ _____

☐ _____

DAILY GRATITUDE

☐ _____

☐ _____

☐ _____

GOOD LISTENING

S M T W T F S ☐

» The theme this week is "Good Listening" because it requires practice, discipline, and curiosity in order to become good at listening.

Today, practice taking two long breaths before answering a question. Did this practice change your approach or emotion when answering?

TOP THREE TO-DO

☐ _____

☐ _____

☐ _____

DAILY GRATITUDE

☐ _____

☐ _____

☐ _____

GOOD LISTENING

S M T W T F S ☐

>> How do you make time to listen? Do you consciously signal to your employee that you are ready to listen?

Listening is offered from the perspective of humility and servant leadership. How can we use our listening to serve those we serve as leaders?

TOP THREE TO-DO

☐ _____
☐ _____
☐ _____

DAILY GRATITUDE

☐ _____
☐ _____
☐ _____

GOOD LISTENING

>> Listening, and truly hearing, is an act of generosity. Generosity brings joy but also returns the favor.

Listening helps us understand the other person's perspective. What questions can you ask to further your understanding of their perspective?

TOP THREE TO-DO

☐ _____

☐ _____

☐ _____

DAILY GRATITUDE

☐ _____

☐ _____

☐ _____

GOOD LISTENING

>> Listening and leadership go hand in hand. Are you listening to understand the problem? Are you listening to coach? What is your intent when you listen?

What actions can you take that support your listening and understanding? Is it standing? Sitting? Taking notes?

TOP THREE TO-DO

☐ _____

☐ _____

☐ _____

DAILY GRATITUDE

☐ _____

☐ _____

☐ _____

GOOD LISTENING

>> Leaders often have favorite "prodding questions," but if you ask the same questions, you may always get the same results. For good listening and new perspectives, ask new questions.

When is the last time you asked your team members what they are thinking? Do you hear their obstacles? Do you hear their challenges?

TOP THREE TO-DO

☐ _____

☐ _____

☐ _____

DAILY GRATITUDE

☐ _____

☐ _____

☐ _____

STRENGTH IN NATURE
leadership journal

GOOD LISTENING

>> Do you listen "between the words?" In music, the rests or spaces between the notes are as important as the notes. How much more important are the spaces in a conversation?

When you listen, do you listen to respond or do you listen to understand? Consider one interaction recently where a manager extended the availability of trying to understand what you were saying. How did this make you feel?

TOP THREE TO-DO

☐ _____

☐ _____

☐ _____

DAILY GRATITUDE

☐ _____

☐ _____

☐ _____

GOOD LISTENING

» Listening is more than the physical act of hearing sound: it demands deep understanding, curiosity, and a multitude of senses.

What are you hearing today?

TOP THREE TO-DO

☐ _____

☐ _____

☐ _____

DAILY GRATITUDE

☐ _____

☐ _____

☐ _____

STRENGTH IN NATURE

GOOD LISTENING

» When you speak, when you listen, do you invite the other person in by using your words, with energy, and body language?

Who do you enjoy listening to? Do you love their words? Their combination of words? Or their message? Understanding what resonates with you when listening to others guides you to find your own voice.

TOP THREE TO-DO

☐ _____

☐ _____

☐ _____

DAILY GRATITUDE

☐ _____

☐ _____

☐ _____

GOOD LISTENING

S M T W T F S

>> Just breathe! Listening is sometimes hard because we may feel defensive. Open yourself to the message to grow as a leader and to grow the relationship with your employee.

In the face of challenging feedback, what good listening skills do you practice to keep calm?

TOP THREE TO-DO

- [ ] _____
- [ ] _____
- [ ] _____

DAILY GRATITUDE

- [ ] _____
- [ ] _____
- [ ] _____

STRENGTH IN NATURE
leadership series

Highlights

*What are the **top three concepts** you learned from each element?*

*How will you **carry these habits forward** in your leadership practice?*

FRIENDLINESS   LEARNED   DO

☐ _____   ☐ _____

☐ _____   ☐ _____

☐ _____   ☐ _____

POSITIVITY

☐ _____   ☐ _____

☐ _____   ☐ _____

☐ _____   ☐ _____

AVAILABILITY

☐ _____   ☐ _____

☐ _____   ☐ _____

☐ _____   ☐ _____

GOOD LISTENING

☐ _____   ☐ _____

☐ _____   ☐ _____

☐ _____   ☐ _____

Thank You

WHAT COMES NEXT

Congratulations! You have just completed Likeable Leadership Journal 2. The third and final journal in this series includes celebrating victories. There is no need to wait for Journal 3. You can celebrate your hard work now.

You are well on your way to becoming the best you, a leader, and a lifelong learner. Successful learners apply what they have learned in practice. To continue building your leadership skills, focus on the skills you highlighted on the last pages of Journals 1 and 2. Reflect on how you can refine these skills as you practice leadership. To learn more, go to www.strengthinnature.com/likeableleadership.

Leadership begins with an understanding of self and moves into the realm of interactions with others. These reflection exercises support your leadership development to reach your goals. Aim high and share your success stories with me! I would love to celebrate your success. Thank you for allowing me to continue to be a part of your leadership journey. I look forward to hearing from you as you complete Journal 3.

NOTES

NOTES